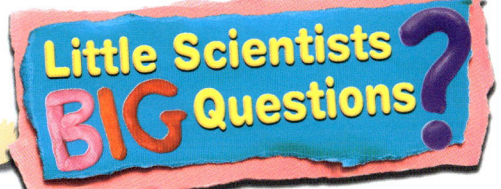

How Does a Vet Use Science?

By **Ruth Owen**

Design by **Alix Wood**

Today, we are visiting the vet with our pets.

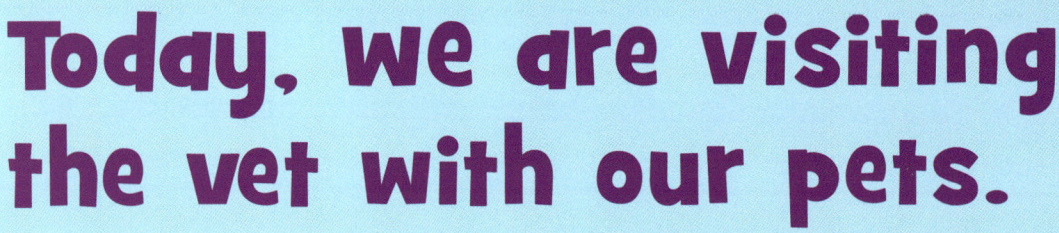

My claws are too long.

I need an injection.

My mouth hurts.

Vets are doctors who take care of animals.

This dog is in hospital.

Vet

They work in an animal hospital called a surgery.

Vets are kind and caring and very good at science.

How does a vet use science?

Come on little scientists, let's answer that BIG question!

A vet asks the animal's owner lots of questions.

Is the animal eating?

Can the animal poo and wee?

Does the animal want to play?

Does the animal seem tired?

All scientists ask questions. Then they do investigations to answer their questions.

Let's Investigate!

A vet listens to an animal's heart and breathing with a stethoscope.

Stethoscope

Let's say it!
"STETH-uh-skope"

A healthy dog's heart should beat 80 to 120 times per minute.

A vet takes an animal's temperature with a thermometer.

Thermometer

A vet uses an otoscope to look into an animal's ears.

A vet must know all about anatomy.

An animal's anatomy is its bones, muscles and other body parts.

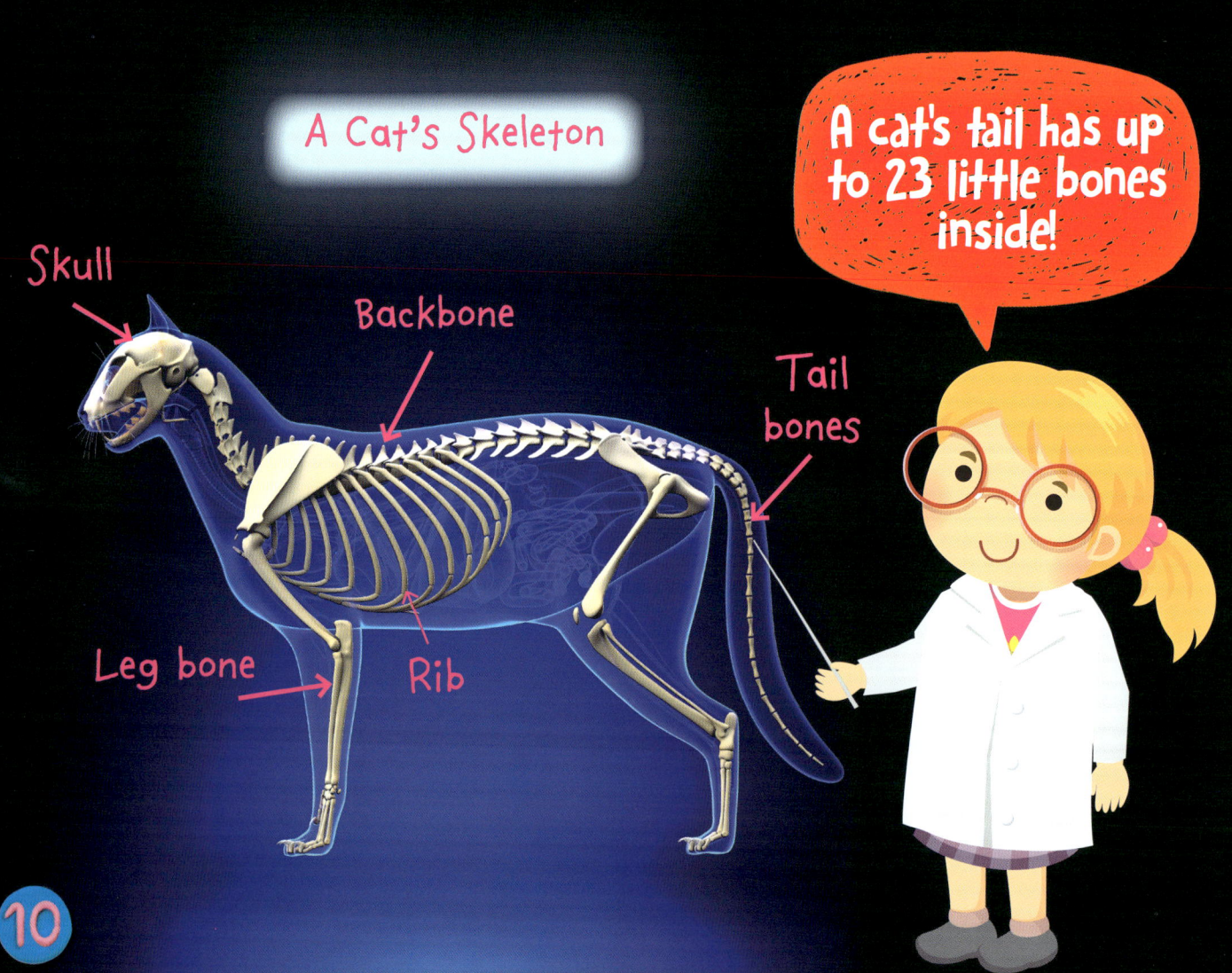

A Cat's Skeleton

Skull
Backbone
Tail bones
Leg bone
Rib

A cat's tail has up to 23 little bones inside!

A vet must know the anatomy of lots of different animals.

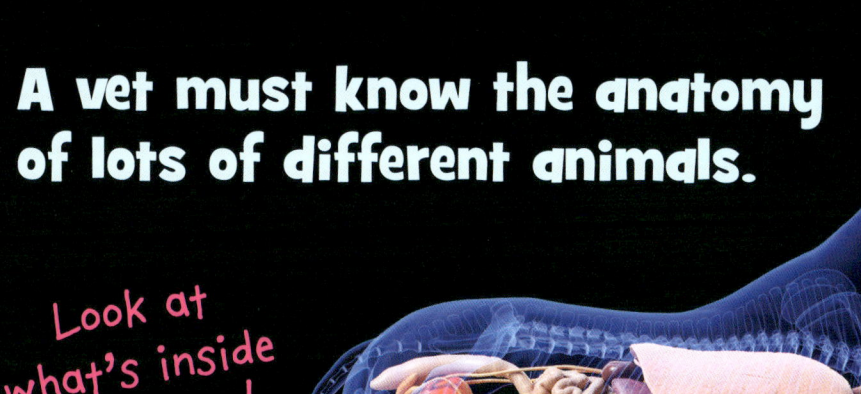

Look at what's inside this horse!

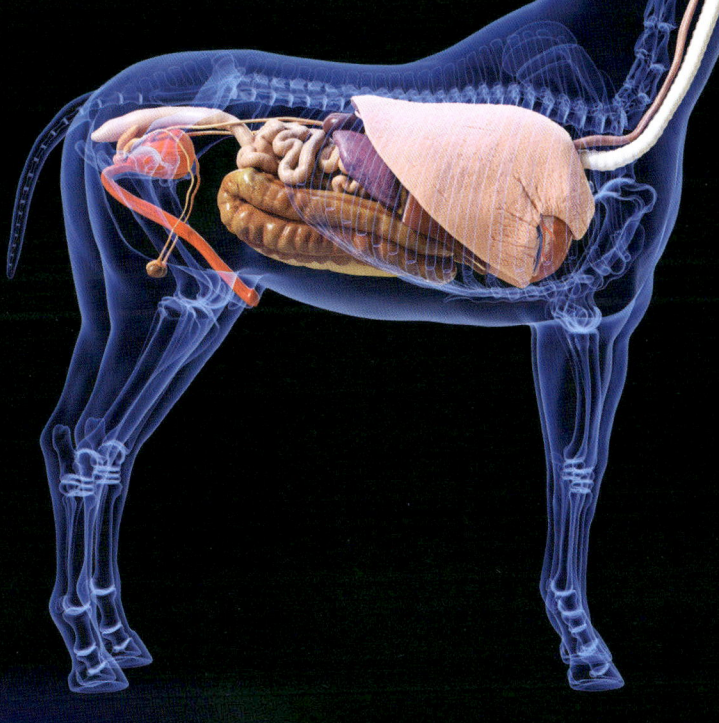

A dog's muscles

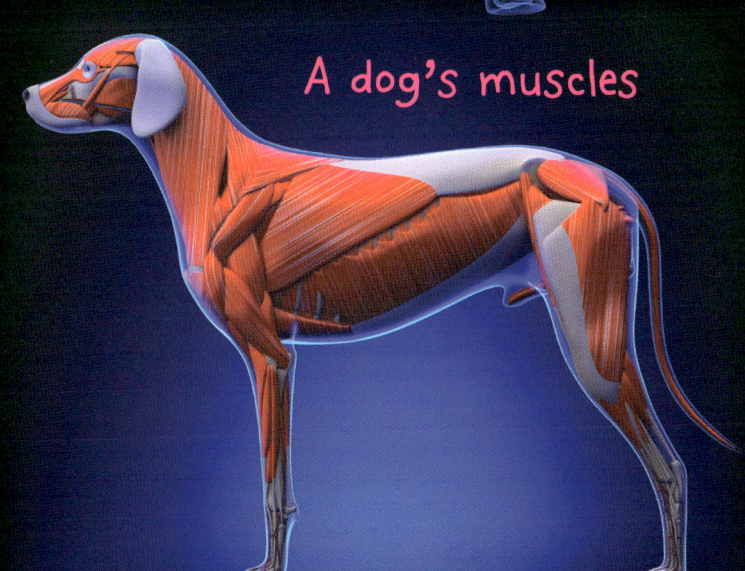

A tortoise's skeleton

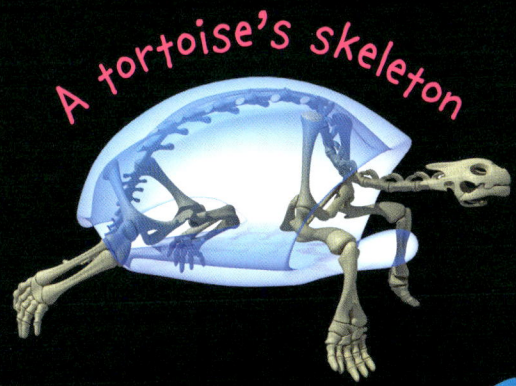

An X-ray machine is used to take a picture of what's inside an animal's body.

A vet gives the animal a special injection, so it is sleepy and doesn't move.

Technician

X-ray machine

A vet has important helpers called nurses and technicians.

A vet also uses an ultrasound machine to see inside animals.

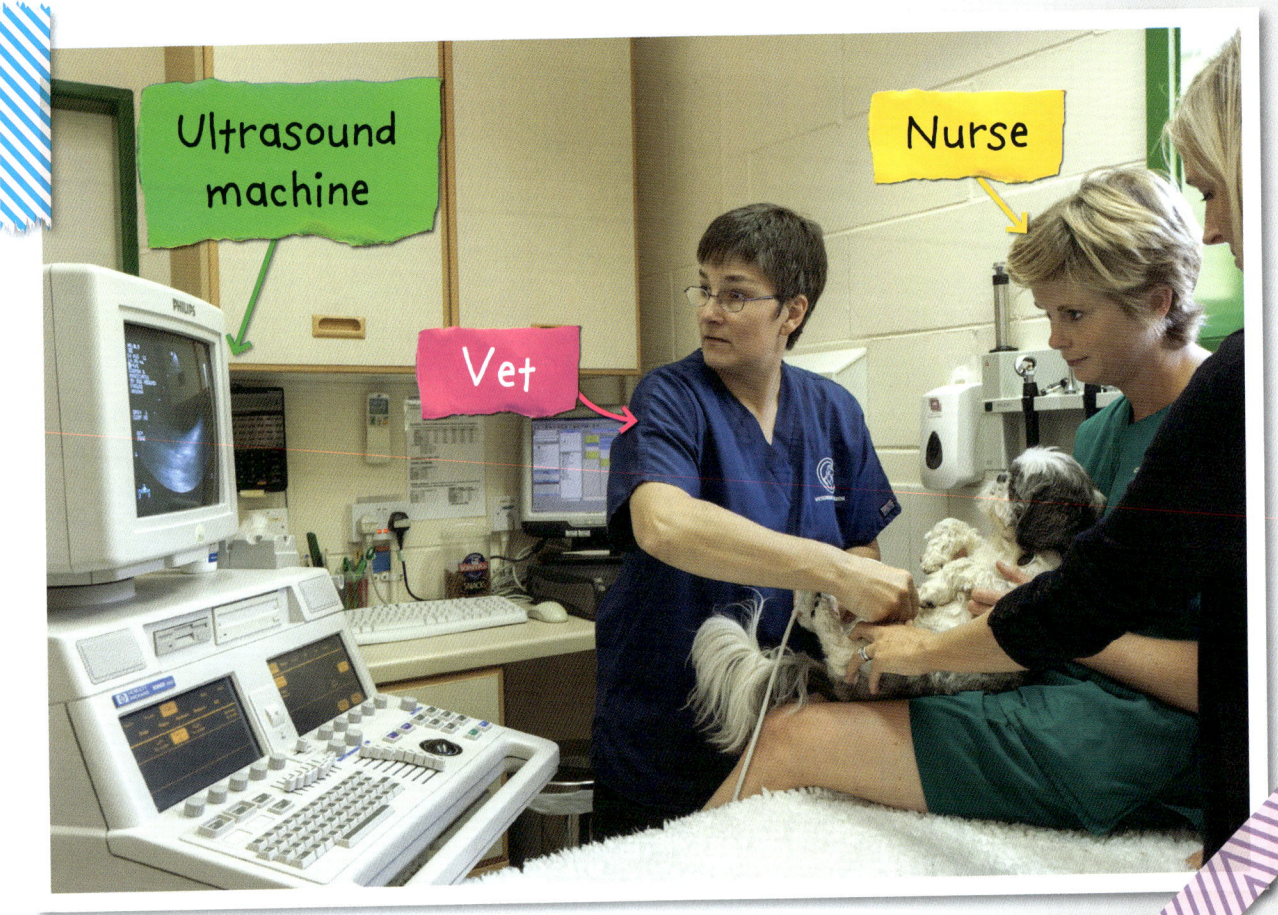

Ultrasound machine

Nurse

Vet

The vet puts a part called a probe on the dog's tummy.

Sometimes poo can show a vet why an animal is ill.

This poor kitty is in the animal hospital.

A nurse collects some of the kitten's poo.

A technician looks at a tiny bit of poo under a microscope.

The kitten is ill because she has roundworms living in her stomach.

Roundworm

The technician can see the wiggly worms in the poo.

The vet will give the kitten medicine to kill the worms.

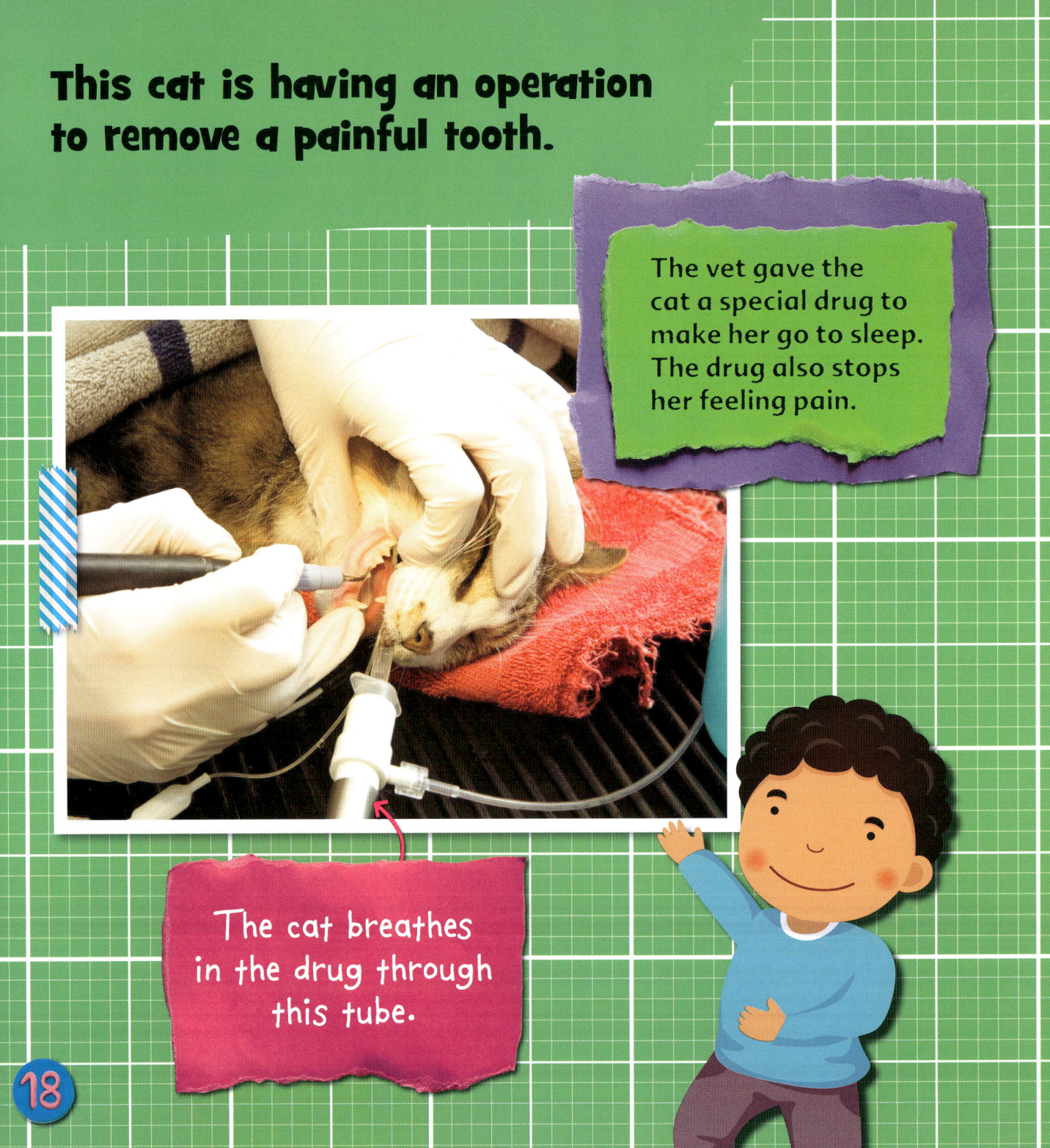

This cat is having an operation to remove a painful tooth.

The vet gave the cat a special drug to make her go to sleep. The drug also stops her feeling pain.

The cat breathes in the drug through this tube.

After an operation the animal is put in a hospital cage.

A nurse puts a warm blanket over the cat.

She will soon be ready to go home!

Sometimes vets use their science skills to help big animals on farms.

A vet is also an animal dentist.

Open wide!

Some vets take care of the animals in zoos.

Zoo vet

Red panda cub

A vet uses maths to carefully measure how much medicine to put in an injection.

Vets help us take care of our pets.

The vet injects a microchip with a special number into this puppy.

Special needle

Microchip

If the puppy gets lost and then found, a vet can read the number with a machine.

The number tells the vet where the lost puppy lives!

Vets and nurses clip animal toenails. Long toenails can hurt an animal's feet.

The vet gives the rabbit an injection called a vaccination. It will stop him catching nasty rabbit diseases.

Let's say it! "vak-suh-NAY-shun"

Now we know how vets use science. Good work, little scientists!

My Science Words

anatomy
All the parts of a living thing. An animal's anatomy includes its bones, muscles, heart and stomach.

investigation
A careful look at something to discover facts about it.

temperature
How hot or cold something is. An animal's temperature shows a vet if the animal is healthy or ill.

vaccination
A special medicine or injection that stops an animal or person getting a disease.

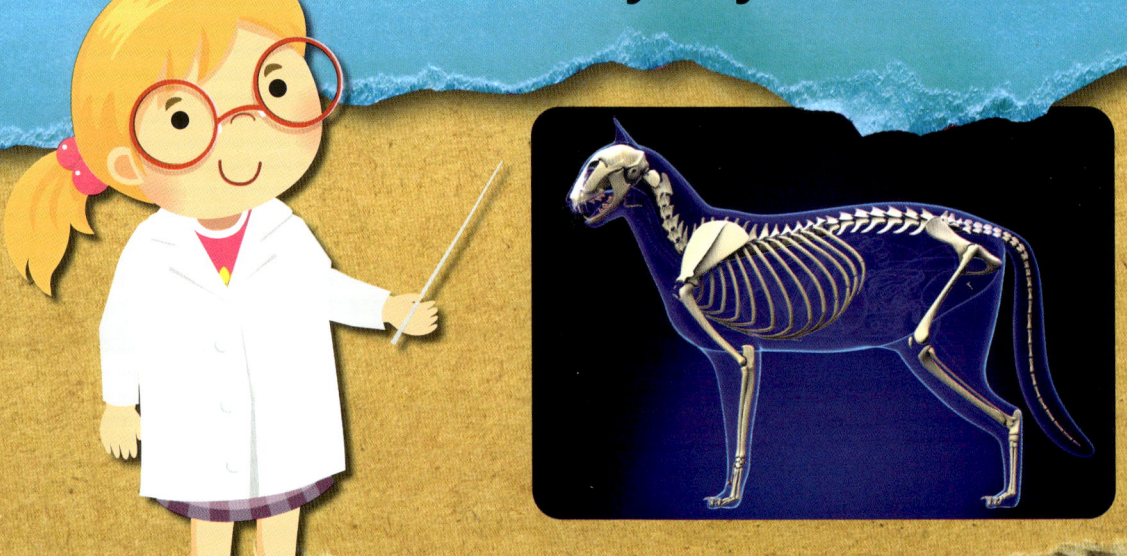